Valentines

The Very Best In Modern Love Songs

Project Manager: Sy Feldman
Book Design: Jorge Paredes

VALENTINE

Composed by
JIM BRICKMAN and JACK KUGELL

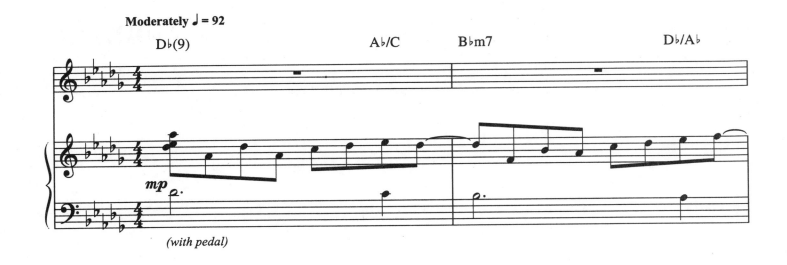

Valentine - 6 - 1

4

FOOLISH GAMES

Words and Music by
JEWEL KILCHER

Moderately slow ♩ = 66

(with pedal)

Verse:

1. You took your coat off and stood in the rain,
2.3.4. See additional lyrics

you're al-ways cra-zy like that. And I watched from my win-dow, al-ways felt I was

* Vocal sung one octave lower

Verse 2:
You're always the mysterious one with
Dark eyes and careless hair,
You were fashionably sensitive
But too cool to care.
You stood in my doorway with nothing to say
Besides some comment on the weather.
(To Pre-Chorus:)

Verse 3:
You're always brilliant in the morning,
Smoking your cigarettes and talking over coffee.
Your philosophies on art, Baroque moved you.
You loved Mozart and you'd speak of your loved ones
As I clumsily strummed my guitar.

Verse 4:
You'd teach me of honest things,
Things that were daring, things that were clean.
Things that knew what an honest dollar did mean.
I hid my soiled hands behind my back.
Somewhere along the line, I must have gone
Off track with you.

Pre-Chorus 2:
Excuse me, think I've mistaken you for somebody else,
Somebody who gave a damn, somebody more like myself.
(To Chorus:)

BECAUSE YOU LOVED ME
(Theme from "Up Close & Personal")

Words and Music by
DIANE WARREN

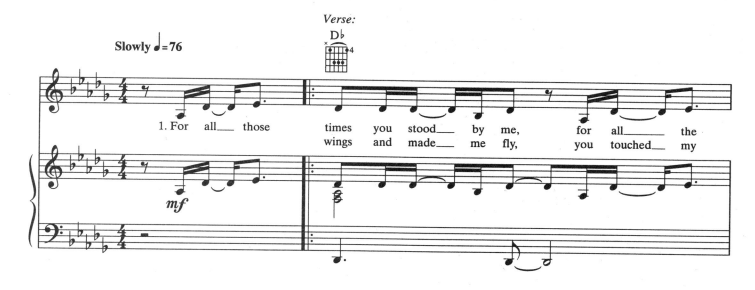

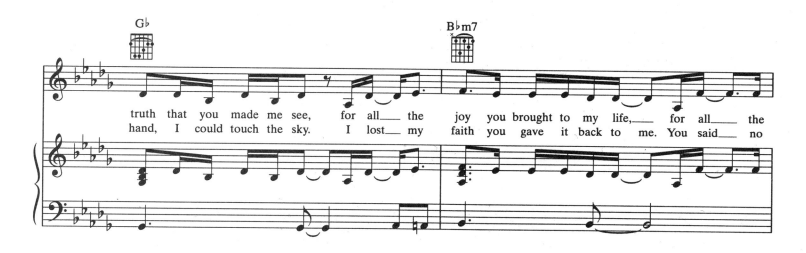

Because You Loved Me - 5 - 1

From the Touchstone Motion Picture "CON AIR"

HOW DO I LIVE

Words and Music by
DIANE WARREN

How Do I Live - 4 - 1

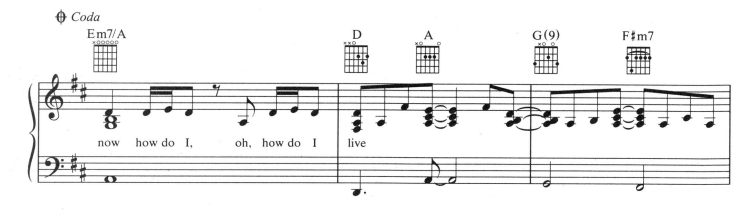

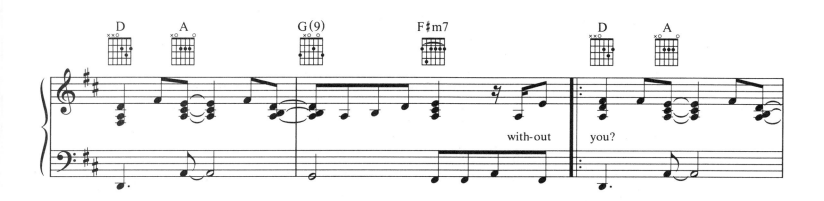

F♯m7
G♯m7
C♯m7
Em7/A
ba - by, you would take a - way ev - 'ry - thing
good in my life.
And tell me
Chorus:
D
A
G
F♯m7
D
A
now, how do I live with - out
you? I want to know.
How do I breathe with - out
G
F♯m7
Bm7
Em7
F♯m7
G(9)
you, if you ev - er go?
How do I ev - er,
ev - er sur - vive?
To Coda
1.
Em7/A
D
F♯m7/B
How do I,
how do I, oh, how do I
live?
2. With - out you,
2.
Em7/A
D
F♯m
Em7
how do I, oh, how do I
live?

*Repeat ad lib. and fade
(vocal 1st time only)*

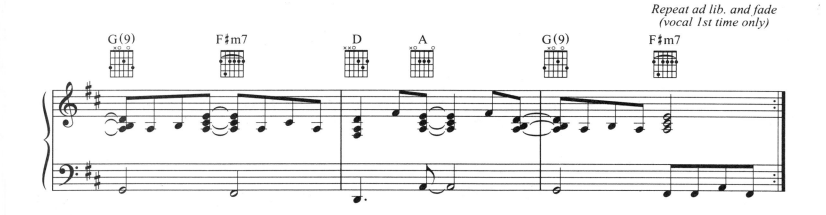

Verse 2:
Without you, there'd be no sun in my sky,
There would be no love in my life,
There'd be no world left for me.
And I, baby, I don't know what I would do,
I'd be lost if I lost you.
If you ever leave,
Baby, you would take away everything real in my life.
And tell me now...
(To Chorus:)

From the Original Soundtrack Album "THE PREACHER'S WIFE"

I BELIEVE IN YOU AND ME

Words and Music by
SANDY LINZER and DAVID WOLFERT

Verse 2:
I will never leave your side,
I will never hurt your pride.
When all the chips are down,
I will always be around,
Just to be right where you are, my love.
Oh, I love you, boy.
I will never leave you out,
I will always let you in
To places no one has ever been.
Deep inside, can't you see?
I believe in you and me.
(To Bridge:)

UN-BREAK MY HEART

Words and Music by
DIANE WARREN

YOU WERE MEANT FOR ME

Words and Music by
JEWEL KILCHER and STEVE POLTZ

You Were Meant for Me - 5 - 1

Verse 2:
I called my mama, she was out for a walk.
Consoled a cup of coffee, but it didn't wanna talk.
So I picked up a paper, it was more bad news,
More hearts being broken or people being used.
Put on my coat in the pouring rain.
I saw a movie, it just wasn't the same,
'Cause it was happy and I was sad,
And it made me miss you, oh, so bad.
(To Chorus:)

Verse 3:
I brush my teeth and put the cap back on,
I know you hate it when I leave the light on.
I pick a book up and then I turn the sheets down,
And then I take a breath and a good look around.
Put on my pj's and hop into bed.
I'm half alive but I feel mostly dead.
I try and tell myself it'll be all right,
I just shouldn't think anymore tonight.
(To Chorus:)

KISSING YOU
(Love Theme From "ROMEO + JULIET")

Words and Music by
DES'REE and TIM ATACK

Moderately slow ♩. = 112

1. Pride_ can stand a thou-sand tri - als, the

strong_ will nev - er fall. But watch - ing stars_ with-out_ you, my_ soul cried._____

Chorus:

ANGEL EYES

Composed by
JIM BRICKMAN

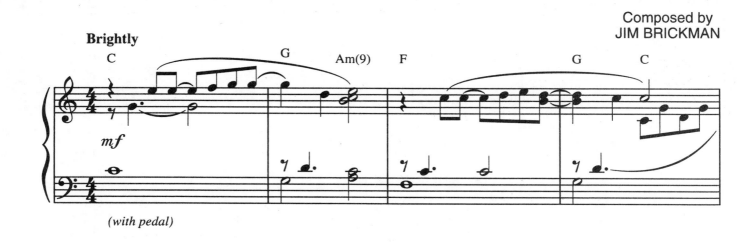

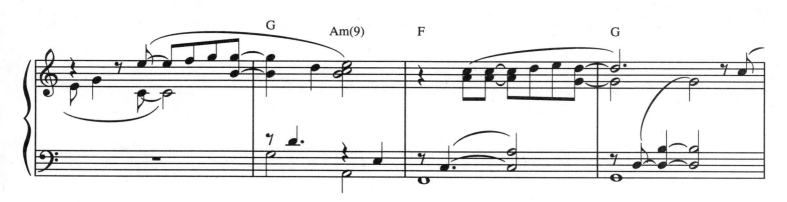

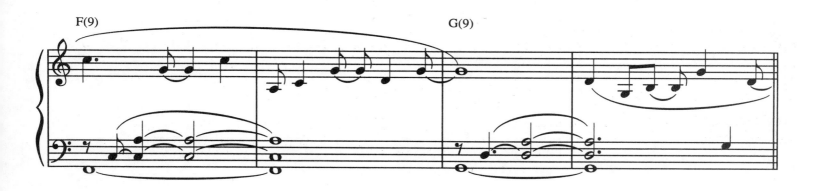

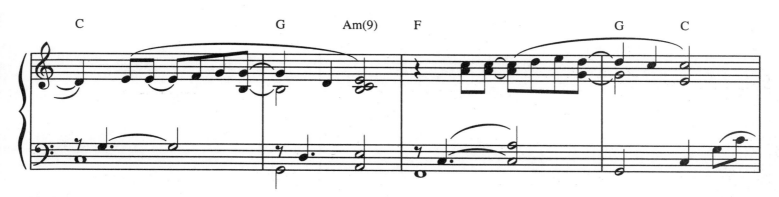

Angel Eyes - 5 - 1

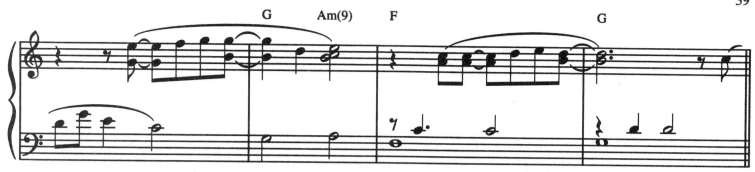

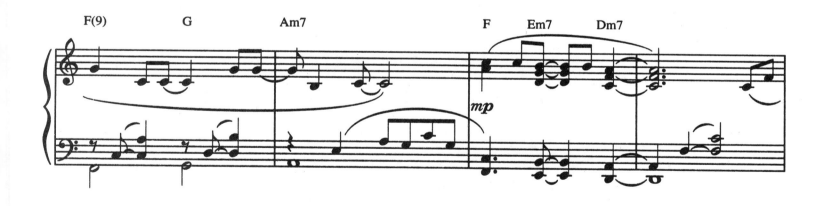

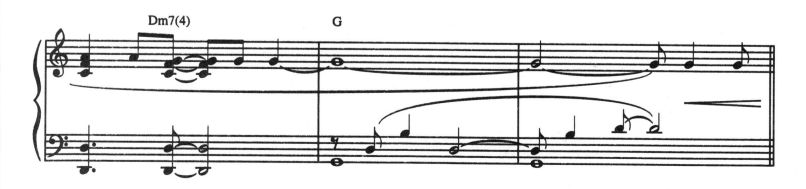

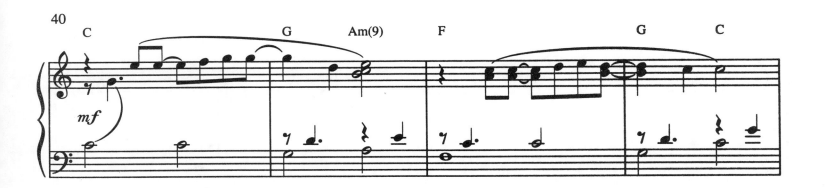

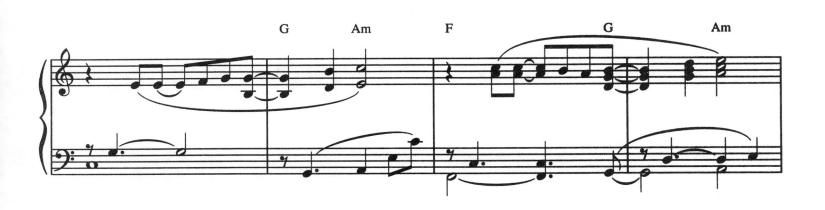

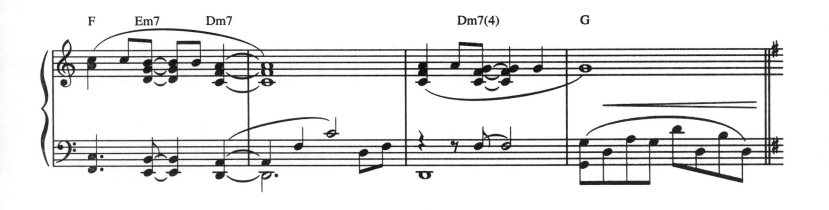

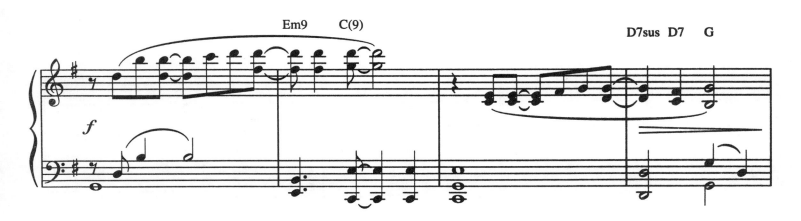

ME AND YOU

Words and Music by
SKIP EWING and RAY HERNDON

Me and You - 3 - 1

Verse 5:
Ordinary?
No, really don't think so.
Just a precious few
Ever make it last,
Get as lucky as
Me and you.

I DO

Words and Music by
PAUL BRANDT

And did I say___ my love___ is true?___ Ba-by, I

dim.

1. will, I am,___ I can,___ I have,___ I do.___

2. will, I am,___ I can,___ I have, I do.___

mp

mf (Instrumental solo...

Verse 3:
I know the time will disappear,
But this love we're building on will always be here.
No way that this is sinking sand,
On this solid rock we'll stand forever...
(To Chorus:)

AS LONG AS YOU LOVE ME

By MAX MARTIN

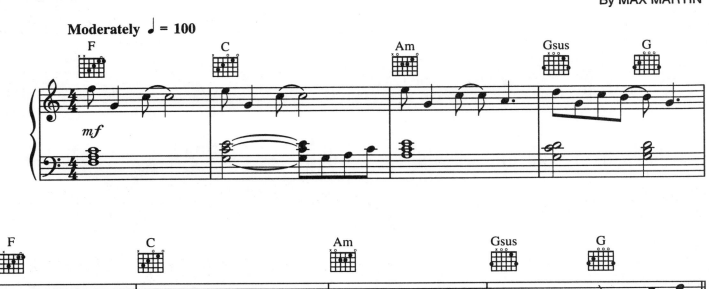

1. Al-though

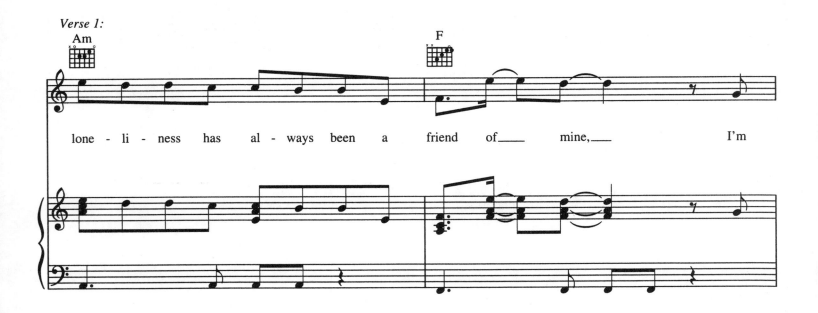

lone-li-ness has al-ways been a friend of___ mine,___ I'm

THE WIND BENEATH MY WINGS

Words and Music by
LARRY HENLEY and JEFF SILBAR

Gently flowing, in 2

It must have been cold there in my shad - ow, ___

to nev - er have sun - light on your

The Wind Beneath My Wings - 7 - 1

62

The Wind Beneath My Wings - 7 - 6

WEDDING SONG
(There Is Love)

© 1971, 1994 PUBLIC DOMAIN FOUNDATION, INC.
431 South Palm Canyon Dr., Palm Springs, Calif. 92262

Wedding Song - 3 - 2

I CROSS MY HEART

Words and Music by
STEVE DORFF and ERIC KAZ

I Cross My Heart - 5 - 1

Additional Lyrics

2. You will always be the miracle
   That makes my life complete.
   And as long as there's a breath in me
   I'll make yours just as sweet.
   As we look into the future,
   It's as far as we can see.
   So let's make each tomorrow
   Be the best that it can be.
   (To Chorus)

From the Motion Picture "THE MIRROR HAS TWO FACES"

I FINALLY FOUND SOMEONE

Words and Music by
BARBRA STREISAND, MARVIN HAMLISCH,
R.J. LANGE and BRYAN ADAMS

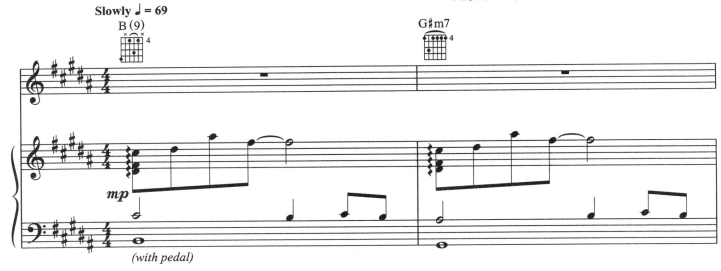

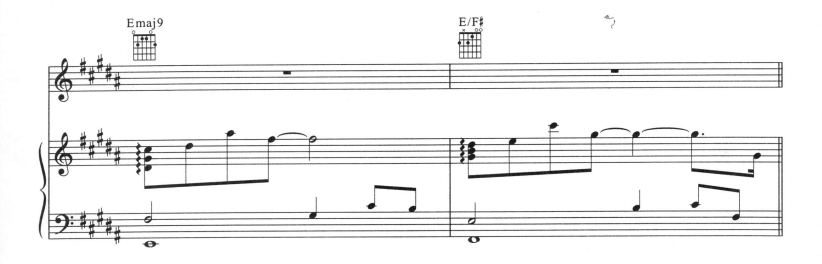

I Finally Found Someone - 8 - 1

I fi-n'lly found the one___ that makes me feel com-plete.

It start-ed o-ver cof - fee, we start-ed out as friends.

It's fun-ny how, from sim-ple things,___ the best things be - gin.___

___ This time, it's dif-f'rent, it's all be-cause of you.___

ev - er I do,_____ it's just got to be____ you. Ooh, my

life has just be - gun,_____ I fi - n'lly

found some - one._____

I WILL ALWAYS LOVE YOU

Words and Music by
DOLLY PARTON

I Will Always Love You - 5 - 1

Verse 3: Instrumental solo

Verse 4:
I hope life treats you kind
And I hope you have all you've dreamed of.
And I wish to you, joy and happiness.
But above all this, I wish you love.
(To Chorus:)

FOR YOU I WILL

Words and Music by
DIANE WARREN

For You I Will - 5 - 1

I LOVE YOU ALWAYS FOREVER

Words and Music by
DONNA LEWIS

"I Love You Always Forever" is inspired by the H.E. Bates novel *"Love for Lydia."*
Chorus/Bridge lyric courtesy of *Michael Joseph Ltd.* and *The Estate of H.E. Bates.*

I love you, al - ways for-ev - er, near and far, clos - er to-geth - er.

Ev - ery-where, I__ will be with you, ev - ery-thing, I__ will do for you. I love you, al - ways for-ev - er,

Repeat ad lib. and fade

near and far, clo - ser to-geth-er. Ev - ery-where, I__ will be with you, ev - ery-thing, I__ will do for you.

Verse 3:
You've got the most unbelievable blue eyes I've ever seen.
You've got me almost melting away as we lay there
Under blue sky with pure white stars,
Exotic sweetness, a magical time.
(To Chorus:)

SAVE THE BEST FOR LAST

Words and Music by
WENDY WALDMAN, JON LIND
and PHIL GALDSTON

Save the Best for Last - 5 - 1

TELL HIM

Words and Music by
LINDA THOMPSON, DAVID FOSTER
and WALTER AFANASIEFF

Tell Him - 6 - 1

out to him___ and whis - per, whis - per words so soft and sweet.

Barbra: Hold him close to feel his heart beat. *Celine:* Love will___ be the gift you give your - self.___

___ Ooh,_____ mm, mm._____ *Both:* Nev - er let him go.

Verse 2:
(Barbra:)
Touch him with the gentleness you feel inside. *(C: I feel it.)*
Your love can't be denied.
The truth will set you free.
You'll have what's meant to be.
All in time, you'll see.
(Celine:)
I love him, *(B: Then show him.)*
Of that much I can be sure. *(B: Hold him close to you.)*
I don't think I could endure
If I let him walk away
When I have so much to say.
(To Chorus:)

I WILL COME TO YOU

Words and Music by
ISAAC HANSON, TAYLOR HANSON,
ZACHARY HANSON, BARRY MANN
and CYNTHIA WEIL

Chorus:

When you have no light to guide you, and no one to walk be-side you, I will

come to you, oh, come to you.
come to you, oh, I will come to you.

When the

night is dark and storm-y, you won't have to reach out for me, I will

I Will Come to You - 6 - 1

I Will Come to You - 6 - 2

1.
G♭/A♭
A♭
2.
G♭/A♭
A♭
what may. When you what may. When the
D♭
A♭
E♭m
B♭m
night is dark and storm-y, you won't have to reach out for me, oh, I will
G♭
E♭m7/A♭
D♭
come to you, oh, I will come to you, oh.
Bridge:
E♭m7
B♭m
We all need some-bod-y we can turn to, oh,

SOMETHING ABOUT THE WAY
YOU LOOK TONIGHT

Lyrics by
BERNIE TAUPIN

Music by
ELTON JOHN

Something About the Way You Look Tonight - 4 - 4

(EVERYTHING I DO) I DO IT FOR YOU

From The Motion Picture "Robin Hood: Prince Of Thieves"

Written by
BRYAN ADAMS, ROBERT JOHN LANGE
and MICHAEL KAMEN

Look in-to my eyes,___ you will see___
Look in-to your heart,___ you will find___ there's

what you mean to ___ me. Search your heart,___ search your
noth - ing there to ___ hide. So, take me as I am, take my

(Everything I Do) I Do It for You - 4 - 1

(Everything I Do) I Do It for You - 4 - 4

WHERE'S THE LOVE

Words and Music by
ISAAC HANSON, TAYLOR HANSON,
ZACHARY HANSON, MARK HUDSON
and STEVEN SALOVER

KILLING ME SOFTLY WITH HIS SONG

Words by
NORMAN GIMBEL

Music by
CHARLES FOX

Moderately slow ♩ = 92

Chorus:

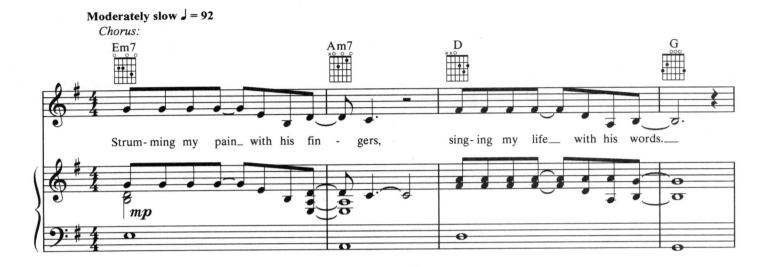

Strum-ming my pain__ with his fin - gers, sing-ing my life__ with his words.__

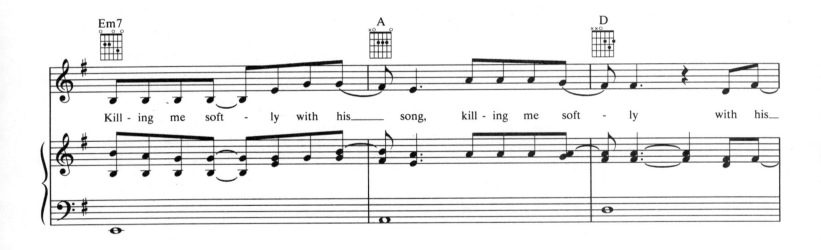

Kill-ing me soft-ly with his__ song, kill-ing me soft - ly with his__

__ song. Tell - ing my whole__ life with his__ words. Kill - ing me__

F
E
soft - ly with his song.
N.C.
Ooh, do do do do do do.
Ooh, do do do Ooh.

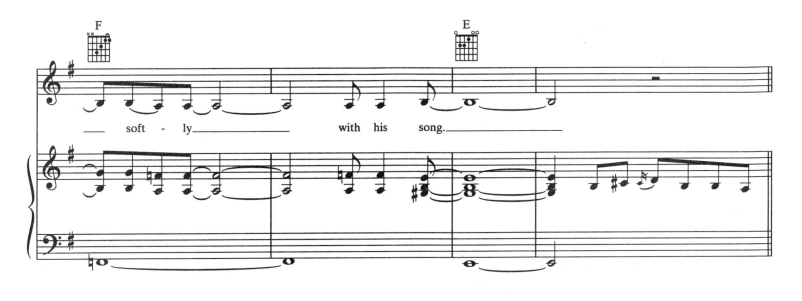

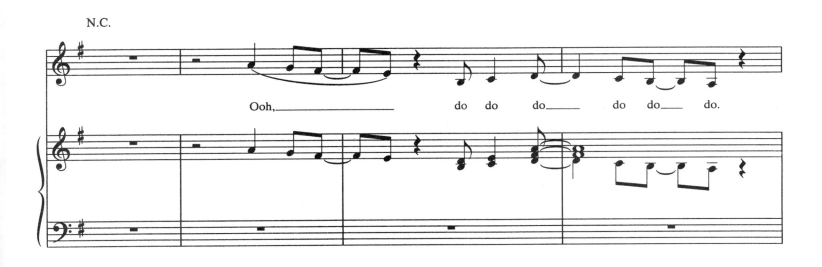

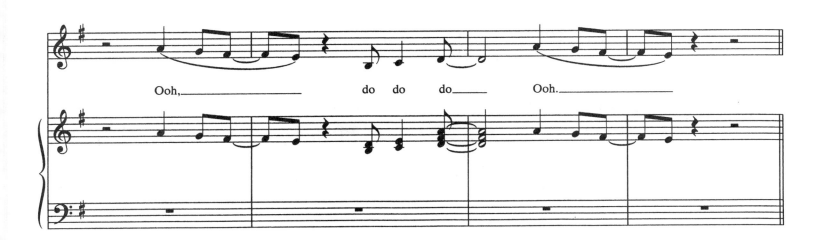

Verse:
N.C.

1. I heard he sang___ a good___ song, I heard he had___ a style.___
2. I felt all flush___ with fe - ver, em - bar - rassed by___ the crowd.___

And so I came___ to see___ him to lis - ten___ for a while.___
I felt he found___ my let - ters and read each___ one out loud.___

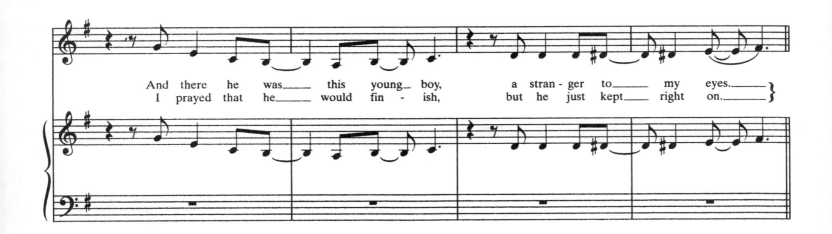

And there he was___ this young___ boy, a stran - ger to___ my eyes.___
I prayed that he___ would fin - ish, but he just kept___ right on.___

BUTTERFLY KISSES

Words and Music by
BOB CARLISLE and RANDY THOMAS

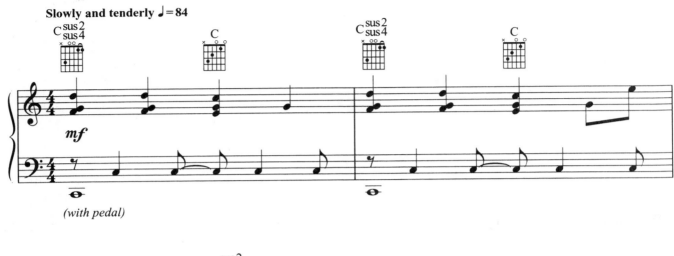

(with pedal)

1. There's

%% *Verses 1 & 3:*

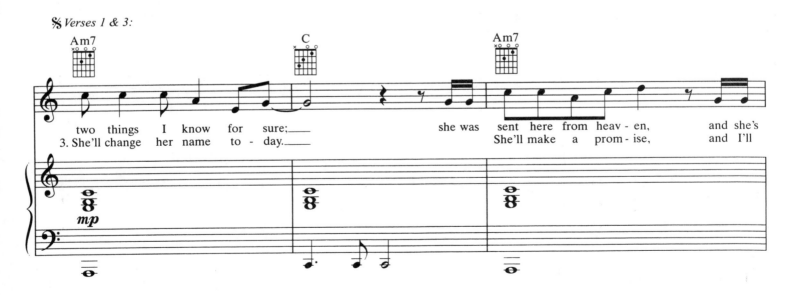

two things   I   know   for   sure;___   she was   sent here from heav - en,   and she's
3. She'll change   her   name   to - day.___   She'll make   a   prom - ise,   and I'll

Butterfly Kisses - 7 - 1

138

love ev-'ry morn - ing and but-ter-fly kiss - es.__ I could-n't ask God__ for more,__ man,

this is what love is.__ I know I've got__ to let__ her go, but I'll al - ways__ re-mem - ber__

ev-'ry hug in the morn - ing and but-ter-fly kiss - es.__

YOU LIGHT UP MY LIFE

Words and Music by
JOE BROOKS

You Light Up My Life - 3 - 1

SAND AND WATER

Words and Music by
BETH NIELSEN CHAPMAN

*Recording is in the key of F♯.

Sand and Water - 4 - 1

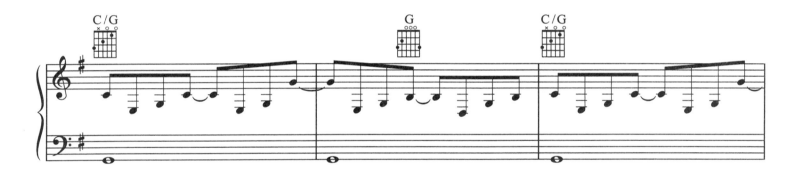

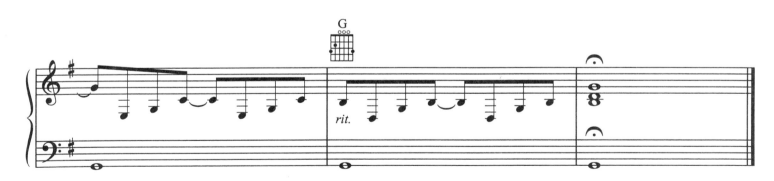

Verses 2 & 4:
All alone I came into this world,
All alone I will someday die.
Solid stone is just sand and water, baby,
Sand and water and a million years gone by.
(To Chorus/Coda:)

Verse 3:
All alone I heal this heart of sorrow,
All alone I raise this child.
Flesh and bone, he's just bursting towards tomorrow,
And his laughter fills my world and wears your smile.
(To Chorus:)

I SWEAR

By
GARY BAKER and FRANK MYERS

Moderately slow

Pedal throughout

(See additional lyrics)

I see the ques - tions in — your eyes, —

— I know what's weigh - ing on — your mind, — but you can be sure —

Additional lyrics

2. I'll give you everything I can,
   I'll build your dreams with these two hands,
   And we'll hang some memories on the wall.
   And when there's silver in your hair,
   You won't have to ask if I still care,
   'Cause as time turns the page my love won't age at all.
   (To Chorus)

From the Twentieth Century-Fox Motion Picture "THE ROSE"

THE ROSE

Words and Music by
AMANDA McBROOM

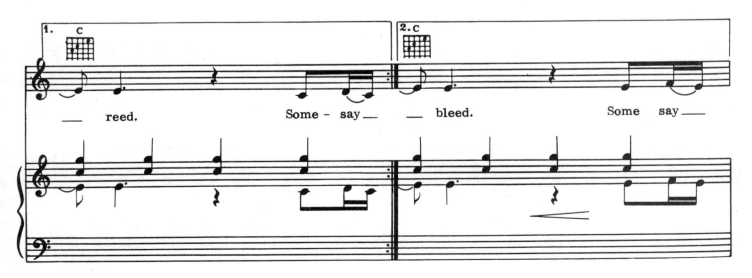

The Rose - 4 - 1

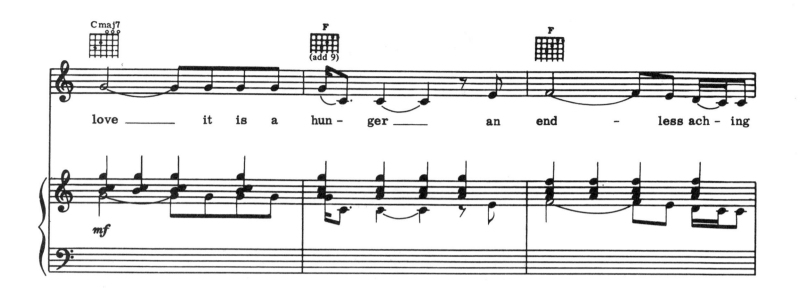

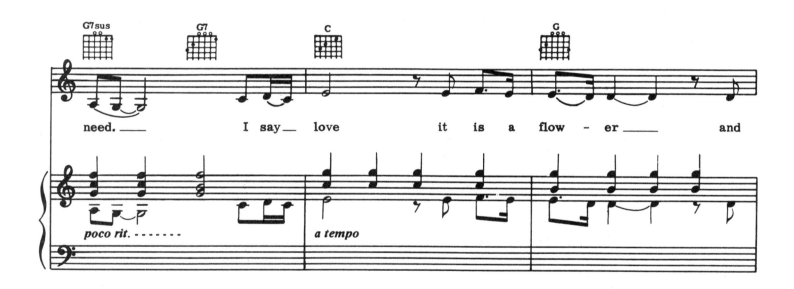

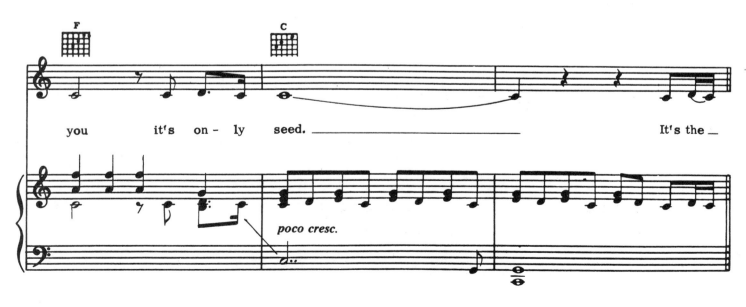

The Rose - 4 - 2

From the Twentieth Century Fox Motion Picture
"ANASTASIA"

AT THE BEGINNING

Lyrics by
LYNN AHRENS

Music by
STEPHEN FLAHERTY

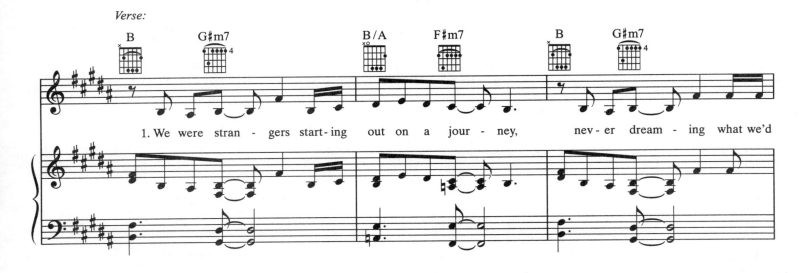

Life is a road, now__ and for-ev-er. Won-der-ful jour - ney! I'll be there when the world stops turn-ing,

I'll be there when the storm is through. In the end, I wan - na be stand-ing at the be-gin-ning with

you.

Verse:

3. We were stran - gers on a

cra-zy ad - ven - ture nev - er dream - ing how our dreams would come true.__ Now

on._____ Start-ing out on a jour-ney. Life is a road, and I want to keep go-ing.

Love is a riv-er, I wan-na keep flow-ing. In the end, I wan-na be stand-ing at the be-gin-ning____

with____ you._____